THE BATTLE OF
VICKSBURG

David C. King

BLACKBIRCH PRESS, INC.

WOODBRIDGE, CONNECTICUT

Published by Blackbirch Press, Inc.
260 Amity Road
Woodbridge, CT 06525

Web site: http://www.blackbirch.com
e-mail: staff@blackbirch.com

Printed in China

10 9 8 7 6 5 4 3 2 1

Photo credits:
Cover, back cover, pages 9, 13–15, 17, 19, 23–24, 30: North Wind Picture Archives; page 7: Corel Corporation; pages 16, 18: National Archives; pages 21, 26, 28: Library of Congress.

Library of Congress Cataloging-in-Publication Data
King, David C.
The Battle of Vicksburg / by David C. King.
        p. cm. — (The Civil War)
Includes index.
        ISBN 1-56711-552-7 (alk. paper)
1. Vicksburg (Miss.)—History—Siege, 1863—Juvenile Literature. [1. Vicksburg (Miss.)—History—Siege, 1863. 2. United States—History—Civil War, 1861-1865—Campaigns.] I. Title. II. Civil War (Blackbirch Press).

E475.27 .K56 2001   2001000724
973. 7'344—dc21

CONTENTS

PREFACE: THE CIVIL WAR

Nearly 150 years after the final shots were fired, the Civil War remains one of the key events in U. S. history. The enormous loss of life alone makes it tragically unique: More Americans died in Civil War battles than in all other American wars combined. More Americans fell at the Battle of Gettysburg than during any battle in American military history. And, in one day at the Battle of Antietam, more Americans were killed and wounded than in any other day in American history.

As tragic as the loss of life was, however, it is the principles over which the war was fought that make it uniquely American. Those beliefs—equality and freedom—are the foundation of American democracy, our basic rights. It was the bitter disagreement about the exact nature of those rights that drove our nation to its bloodiest war.

The disagreements grew in part from the differing economies of the North and South. The warm climate and wide-open areas of the Southern states were ideal for an economy based on agriculture. In the first half of the 19th century, the main cash crop was cotton, grown on large farms called plantations. Slaves, who were brought to the United States from Africa, were forced to do the backbreaking work of planting and harvesting cotton. They also provided the other labor necessary to keep plantations running. Slaves were bought and sold like property, and had been critical to the Southern economy since the first Africans came to America in 1619.

The suffering of African Americans under slavery is one of the great tragedies in American history. And the debate over whether the United States government had the right to forbid slavery—in both Southern states and in new territories—was a dispute that overshadowed the first 80 years of our history.

For many Northerners, the question of slavery was one of morality and not economics. Because the Northern economy was based on manufacturing rather than agriculture, there was little need for slave labor. The primary economic need of Northern states was a protective tax known as a tariff that would make imported goods more expensive than goods made in the North. Tariffs forced Southerners to buy Northern goods and made them economically dependent on the North, a fact that led to deep resentment among Southerners.

Economic control did not matter to the anti-slavery Northerners known as abolitionists. Their conflict with the South was over slavery. The idea that the federal government could outlaw slavery was perfectly reasonable. After all, abolitionists contended, our nation was founded on the idea that all people are created equal. How could slavery exist in such a country?

For the Southern states that joined the Confederacy, the freedom from unfair taxation and the right to make their own decisions about slavery was as important a principle as equality. For most Southerners, the right of states to decide what is best for its citizens was the most important principle guaranteed in the Constitution.

The conflict over these principles generated sparks throughout the decades leading up to the Civil War. The importance of keeping an equal number of slave and free states in the Union became critical to Southern lawmakers in Congress in those years. In 1820, when Maine and Missouri sought admission to the Union, the question was settled by the Missouri Compromise: Maine was admitted as a free state, Missouri as a slave state, thus maintaining a balance in Congress. The compromise stated that all future territories north of the southern boundary of Missouri would enter the Union as free states, those south of it would be slave states.

In 1854, however, the Kansas-Nebraska Act set the stage for the Civil War. That act repealed the Missouri Compromise and, by declaring that the question of slavery should be decided by residents of the territory, set off a rush of pro- and anti-slavery settlers to the new land. Violence between the two sides began almost immediately and soon "Bleeding Kansas" became a tragic chapter in our nation's story.

With Lincoln's election on an anti-slavery platform in 1860, the disagreement over the power of the federal government reached its breaking point. South Carolina became the first state to secede from the Union, followed by Mississippi, Florida, Alabama, Georgia, Louisiana, Virginia, Texas, North Carolina, Tennessee, and Arkansas. Those eleven states became the Confederate States of America. Confederate troops fired the first shots of the Civil War at Fort Sumter, South Carolina, on April 12, 1861. Those shots began a four-year war in which thousands of Americans—Northerners and Southerners—would give, in President Lincoln's words, "the last full measure of devotion."

5

INTRODUCTION: A CITY UNDER SIEGE

 ★ ★ ★ ★ ★

On June 28, 1863, a hot, hazy sun beat down relentlessly on Vicksburg, Mississippi, a city perched high over the mighty Mississippi River. Within its narrow, hilly network of streets, 30,000 Confederate soldiers and 3,000 civilians had been trapped for six terrifying weeks. In front of them, a 70,000-man Union army hemmed in all sides with a steel wall of rifles and cannons. Behind them, on the mile-wide river, a fleet of Federal gunboats made escape impossible.

At first, the city's defenders and citizens had accepted their plight with humor and determination. They managed to joke about the pangs of hunger that grew sharper each day as food supplies dwindled. They became almost oblivious to the constant hailstorm of Union artillery shells that rained on the crumbling city for hours at a time. The Southerners survived on the hope that a Confederate force must be on the way to relieve them.

But no relief column came, and a sense of desperation gripped the defenders. Their greatest enemy now was hunger. Many had already noticed their ankles swelling and their gums bleeding, the first signs of scurvy brought on by malnutrition. And nearly every soldier found that even the lightest work left him weak and exhausted. So, on June 28, an unknown number of men agreed to send a letter to their commander signed "Many Soldiers." The message was brief and bitter: "If you cannot feed us, you had better surrender us, horrible as the idea is, than suffer this noble army to disgrace itself by desertion."

The long struggle for Vicksburg had reached a critical point. The Confederate commander had few options left. Did he dare ask the men to hold on, at least for a few more days? Were they strong enough to try to fight their way out? Or should he surrender the city and the army, knowing that the Confederacy might never recover from such a defeat?

"VICKSBURG IS THE KEY"

From the opening shots of the Civil War at Fort Sumter, S.C., in April 1861, the North—or Union—had two objectives. In the East, the Army of the Potomac would march south from Washington, D.C., and capture Richmond, Virginia, the capital of the Confederacy. In the West, the Union would seize control of the Mississippi River from Illinois to the Gulf of Mexico by capturing Port Hudson, Louisiana.

The North's campaign for Richmond became bogged down from the first battle. Slow-moving Union generals were repeatedly out-maneuvered by their Confederate counterparts. Blue-clad Northern troops usually outnumbered their grey-clad Southern opponents, but could not defeat them. By January 1863, after several defeats, the Union forces were still well short of Richmond.

Union armies in the West were somewhat more successful. Naval gunboats and steamboats helped gain control of the lower Mississippi River, including New Orleans. The North also controlled the upper reaches of the river as far south as Vicksburg, Mississippi. But, from Vicksburg down to Port Hudson, the Confederates continued to have a firm hold on 250 miles of the vital waterway.

On a map, that 250-mile stretch doesn't look like much. But, in the strategy of the Civil War, it was tremendously important. If the Union could gain control of the full length of the Mississippi, the South would be cut in two. The states of Louisiana, Arkansas, and Texas would be isolated from the rest of the Confederacy and unable to supply food or new troops. The North, in turn, would be able to use the river to move men and supplies deep into Southern territory.

President Abraham Lincoln saw the picture clearly. "Vicksburg is the key," the president said. "This war can never be brought to a close until the key is in our pocket . . . ."

Then, in his folksy language, Lincoln explained how Vicksburg provided an important supply link for the South:

8

We may take away all the northern parts of the Confederacy and they can still defy us from Vicksburg. It means hogs and hominy without limit, fresh troops from all the states of the far South, and a cotton country where they can raise that staple without interference.

In Washington, Union General Henry W. Halleck went even further: "In my opinion," he wrote, "the opening of the Mississippi River will be of far more use to us than the capture of forty Richmonds."

The president of the Confederacy, Jefferson Davis, and his generals were well aware how important Vicksburg was to both sides, and they were determined not to let it fall into Union hands. In June 1862, Union naval gunboats and armed steamers tried to bombard the city into submission. It didn't work. The high bluffs of Vicksburg bristled with cannons that fired heavily on the North's ships, forcing them back to New Orleans. In the months that followed, the city's defenders worked tirelessly to make the defenses even stronger against attack from land or the water.

For both North and South, 1863 loomed as the year of decision. Each side knew that the outcome of the campaign for Vicksburg could determine the outcome of the entire war.

Confederate and Union forces battled fiercely for control of the Mississippi River throughout 1862 and much of 1863.

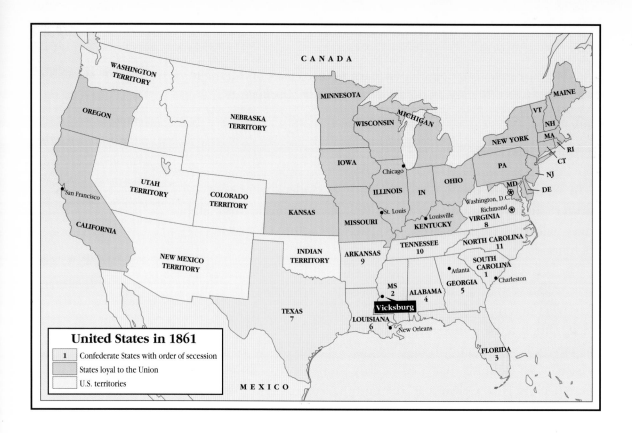

United States in 1861

1	Confederate States with order of secession
	States loyal to the Union
	U.S. territories

Southern Confidence and Northern Gloom

Many Southerners looked forward to 1863 with a good deal of hope and confidence. After nearly two years of warfare, Richmond and Vicksburg remained firmly in Confederate hands. In mid-December 1862, the South's Army of Northern Virginia—led by General Robert E. Lee—soundly beat the much larger Army of the Potomac at the Battle of Fredericksburg. There were now rumors that Lee planned to lead his victorious troops in an invasion of the North, perhaps even in an assault on Washington, D.C., just fifty miles away.

In the West, General Ulysses S. Grant had been given orders to use his army to capture Vicksburg and place the full length of the Mississippi in Union hands. On November 4, 1862, Grant led his huge army south into Mississippi. He never came close to Vicksburg, however, because a Confederate cavalry division circled behind his army and destroyed his supply base. Without food, clothing, and ammunition, Grant could go no further and, late in December, he was forced into a humiliating retreat.

As 1863 began, a chilling gloom settled over the North. The December defeats, East and West, led many to feel that the incredible loss of life on the battlefield was getting them nowhere. The editor of the *Chicago Tribune* predicted that "an armistice is bound to come during the year '63. The Rebs [Confederates] can't be conquered by the present machinery."

January 1, 1863, marked the day that Lincoln's Emancipation Proclamation went into effect. It stated that all slaves in the states still in rebellion were now free. In the long run, the proclamation was to inspire Northerners to fight for two noble causes—restoring the Union and setting free the slaves. But, in this time of gloom in the North, it did little to boost morale. No slaves would be free until Northern victories on the battlefield liberated them from Southern plantations.

In order to achieve a victory in the East, President Lincoln searched for a general to replace Ambrose Burnside as commander of the Army of the Potomac. In the West, however, he resisted calls for Grant's removal. "I think General Grant has hardly a friend left, except myself," the president said. "What I want is [sic] generals who will fight battles and win victories. Grant has done this, and I propose to stand by him."

If Grant hoped to keep the president's support, however, he had to find a way to capture Vicksburg.

Vicksburg: "The Gibraltar of the West"

Vicksburg's geographical position made it almost immune from attack. The bluffs on which it was built loomed more than 200 feet above the Mississippi, making attack from the river impossible. With nearly 100 cannons standing along those cliffs, the defenders controlled the river for a distance of more than 30 miles.

Natural obstacles protected the city as well. From both the north and south, Vicksburg was bordered by miles of swamps, dense thickets, bayous, and twisting rivers. The only approach that offered solid ground for an attacking army was directly from the east, a region of central Mississippi that was still in Confederate hands.

'I think General Grant has hardly a friend left, except myself. What I want is [sic] generals who will fight battles and win victories. Grant has done this, and I propose to stand by him."
—*President Abraham Lincoln*

11

Vicksburg's defenders had made dramatic additions to the defenses that nature provided. On the landward (eastern) side, they had spent nearly a year constructing defenses on a high, curving ridge that extended for nine miles just east of the city's streets. Engineers built watch towers with walls up to twenty feet thick, that overlooked rugged gullies and ravines. There were 115 cannons spaced along this line, and each gun emplacement was protected by trenches and rifle pits. Southerners called Vicksburg the "Gibraltar of the West," a reference to the impregnable rock fortress that guarded the entrance to the Mediterranean Sea.

General Grant had failed in his December 1862 effort to attack the city through central Mississippi. During the early months of 1863, he devised a series of plans for getting his army to the eastern side of Vicksburg. Week after week, his soldiers worked through heavy winter rains with pickaxes and shovels to cut a canal across a hairpin bend in the Mississippi. As they came close to the

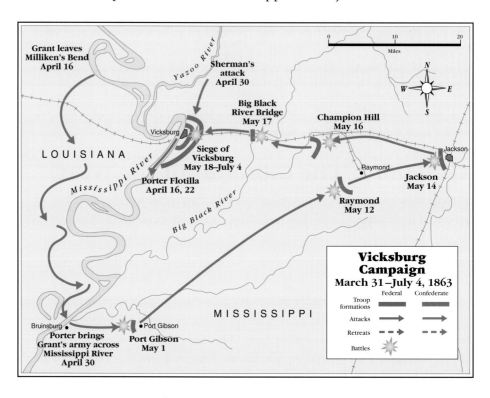

city, they were bombarded by Confederate artillery. Grant then had the men try to create other water routes. Nothing worked. By early April, the general found himself exactly where he had been four months earlier—staring across the river at a seemingly unapproachable Vicksburg.

While newspapers entertained readers with accounts of Grant's waterways, not everyone was amused. One of Grant's critics wrote to a member of Congress:

> *Grant has no plan for taking Vicksburg. He is frittering away time and strength to no purpose. The truth must be told even if it hurts.*

Vicksburg, Mississippi, the city that the Union and Confederate armies fought to control, was set high on a bluff overlooking the Mississippi.

Grant's Risky Plan

In April 1863, Grant devised a new plan for attacking Vicksburg. It was an imaginative scheme, but one so risky that failure could spell disaster for his army and ruin for his career. He presented the idea to his most trusted general, William Tecumseh Sherman, and to Admiral David W. Porter, the ranking naval officer for the northern part of the Mississippi. The plan, he said, was very simple.

First, Porter would lead a risky night passage by a fleet of gunboats, armed steamers, and transport barges beneath the Vicksburg cannons

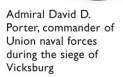

Admiral David D. Porter, commander of Union naval forces during the siege of Vicksburg

to a point about thirty miles south of the city. If enough of the fleet got through, Porter would send a second fleet. These vessels would meet Grant's army, which would have marched down the western (Louisiana) side of the river to the rendezvous point. The second fleet would transport them to the eastern shore of the river. To disguise this movement, Sherman would use part of the army to launch a feint, or false attack, on Vicksburg from the north. As soon as Grant's troops were safely across the river, Sherman would race to join them and they would march swiftly into position to attack the fortress city from the east.

Porter was enthusiastic about the strategy, but Sherman felt that too much could go wrong. Grant insisted they had to go ahead with his plan. "The country is already disheartened over the lack of success on the part of our armies," he said. "The problem for us is to move forward to a decisive victory or our cause is lost."

The Confederates had no idea what Grant was planning, but they felt secure in their fortress city. In April, General John C. Pemberton, the South's commander at Vicksburg, felt so secure that he sent his cavalry division to help a Rebel force in Tennessee and was planning to send an infantry division. On April 11, he sent a telegram to General Joseph Johnston at Jackson, Mississippi, the state capital, that "Grant's forces are being withdrawn to Memphis." And, on April 16, the *Vicksburg Whig* boasted that the North's gunboats ". . . are all more or less damaged, the men dissatisfied and demoralized. . . There is no immediate danger here."

On that night of April 16, the officers and citizens of Vicksburg held a gala ball to celebrate the successful defense of their city. As the party got underway, General Grant was boarding a steamboat at Milliken's Bend, several miles northwest of Vicksburg. With his staff, his wife Julia, and his twelve-year-old son Frederick, Grant planned to watch Porter's fleet try to pass directly through Vicksburg's shoreline defenses.

At about midnight, the Vicksburg party was interrupted by flashes of light and the sound of explosions. Lookouts had spotted Porter's flotilla and quickly lit huge fires to light the river for Confederate artillery.

14

As the Grants watched from a safe distance, a parade of gunboats, steamboats, and transport barges seemed to make painfully slow progress as they steamed past the Vicksburg guns. Porter had "armored" his barges by lashing wet bales of hay to the sides of the gunboats. The Confederate cannons blasted round after round at the seventeen vessels—525 rounds in all—and scored 68 hits. Few of the hits inflicted serious damage. Porter lost only one steamboat and two transports.

Six nights later, Porter sent another flotilla past the Vicksburg batteries, again with the loss of one steamer and several transport barges. In the meantime, Grant had used the six days to lead two of his three army corps down the western side of the Mississippi to their rendezvous with Porter. The first two parts of Grant's plan had worked perfectly.

Late in April, while Sherman led his corps in the feint on Vicksburg from the north, Porter's gunboats and transport barges ferried Grant's army across the mile-wide Mississippi without opposition.

In Enemy Territory

Once joined by Sherman and his corps in early May, Grant had an army of about 33,000 on the eastern side of the river. They were now in enemy territory, cut off from their supply base. Grant had planned for this. He said his troops would "carry what rations of hard bread, coffee, and salt we can and make the country furnish the balance."

Admiral Porter's first flotilla passed the Vicksburg batteries on April 16, 1863.

Ulysses S. Grant, 1822-1885

★ ★ ★ ★ ★

At the start of the Civil War, Ulysses S. Grant was unknown. He became an officer after he graduated from West Point and served in the Mexican War (1846–1848). In February 1862, he became an overnight hero for winning the Union's first two victories at forts Henry and Donelson. Two months later, however, his reputation was tarnished when he was caught off guard at the Battle of Shiloh, which resulted in very high casualties. There were also rumors of Grant's heavy drinking. Grant did drink heavily on occasion, but he also went months at a time without touching alcohol, and never drank during a military campaign.

Grant's troops were unsure of him until the Vicksburg campaign. By then they were accustomed to his ragged appearance, usually clad in a private's badly-worn coat, mud-spattered boots, and only shoulder bars to indicate his rank. Soon men came to feel completely at home with him. After Vicksburg, his troops would follow him anywhere.

In 1864, Grant took command of all Union armies in the final drive to force General Robert E. Lee to surrender. When Lee did surrender at Appomatox Court House in April 1865, Grant revealed how generous he could be. He treated his former enemy with respect, and allowed the Confederate soldiers to take their horses with them so they could use them to plow their fields when they returned home.

Like the Confederates, Union troops made the most of the land, stuffing themselves on ham, pork roasts, sides of bacon, and beef they took from civilian farms.

Despite their dangerous position, the men, and their commander, were in high spirits. After months of frustration, they were thrilled to be in action again. General Grant, constantly on horseback, urging his men on, seemed to be filled with new energy. "None who had known him the previous year could recognize him as being the same man," one of his officers recalled. "From this time on, his genius and his energies seemed to burst forth with new life."

In addition to Sherman's attack north of Vicksburg, Grant used a brilliant cavalry raid to confuse the enemy even more. The raid was led by Colonel Benjamin H. Grierson, who had been a music teacher in Illinois before becoming one of the most daring and successful cavalry officers in either army.

During the last two weeks of April 1863, Grierson led 1,700 Union men on a wild ride through central Mississippi. They tore up fifty miles of railroad track on the three lines that supplied Vicksburg. He sometimes divided the men into smaller groups and struck in different directions to confuse the Confederates even more. Grierson's men won

Porter tied wet bales of hay to the sides of his gunboats for protection.

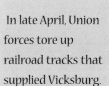

★

In late April, Union forces tore up railroad tracks that supplied Vicksburg.

★

17

several small skirmishes, captured 500 Rebels, and burned many freight cars and train depots. By the time he led his exhausted troops into Union lines at Baton Rouge, Louisiana, they had covered 600 miles in 16 days. They had completely bewildered Rebel commanders Pemberton and Johnston. Grierson's losses were incredibly light, with only three men killed and five wounded.

General Grant, meanwhile, was moving swiftly north and east. At Port Gibson, his army defeated a Confederate force of 5,000 soldiers after a tough, day-long battle. Then, instead of marching directly toward Vicksburg, Grant veered toward Jackson, the capital of Mississippi, forty miles east of Vicksburg.

General William T. Sherman served under Grant at Vicksburg.

Pemberton and Johnston finally saw that Grant was headed to Jackson, the state capital and the source of supplies for Vicksburg. President Davis and Johnston both realized that the only way to stop Grant would be to combine Pemberton's 30,000 men with Johnston's 6,000 at Jackson. Pemberton, however, felt he should "hold Vicksburg as long as possible [because] I still conceive it to be the most important point in the Confederacy."

On May 12, 1863, Grant's lead division met part of Johnston's Rebel army at the town of Raymond, less than fifteen miles from Jackson. Johnston, with only 6,000 Confederates, knew he couldn't defend the state capital and gave orders to evacuate. He wrote a note asking Pemberton to join forces with him by leaving Vicksburg and attacking Grant's army from behind as Grant attempted to move against Jackson. Johnston sent three copies of the note, hoping one would get through. One messenger did get through, but another messenger was a Union spy who delivered his copy to one of Grant's officers.

Consequently, when Pemberton led a 20,000-man force out of Vicksburg on May 16, he did not encounter Grant's supply wagons and rearguard. Instead, he confronted two of Grant's three Union corps ready to do battle. One corps was led by General James McPherson. Another was led by General John McClernand. The third corps, led by Sherman, had already occupied Jackson.

★

Instead of heading directly toward Vicksburg when he crossed the Mississippi, Grant first attacked Jackson, the state capital to the east.

★

John C. Pemberton, 1814-1881

★ ★ ★ ★ ★

Every state in the South saw some of its people fight for the Union, and every Northern state included some men and women who sided with the Confederacy. John C. Pemberton was one of the latter group. Born and raised in Pennsylvania, he sided with the South on many issues and married the daughter of a Virginia plantation-owning family.

Pemberton was a West Point graduate and a career army officer, but he resigned his commission in April 1861 and joined the Confederate army. Although some Southerners questioned his loyalty, he was promoted to the rank of lieutenant general late in 1862 and placed in command of the Vicksburg-Port Hudson region of the Mississippi Valley. After Pemberton surrendered Vicksburg and his Rebel army, the Southern press criticized him severely for allowing his army to be trapped in Vicksburg, disregarding the fact that Union troops had completely surrounded Pemberton.

Southerners were even more outraged that he chose to surrender on the Fourth of July. Some saw this as Pemberton's signal of loyalty to the Union. Pemberton denied these accusations. He resigned his commission and finished the war as a weapons inspector. After the war, Pemberton retired to a farm in Virginia with his family. He later moved to a farm near Philadelphia.

The Battle of Champion Hill, May 16, 1863

Pemberton recovered quickly from the shock of seeing two-thirds of Grant's army advancing toward him. He had his Rebels take up a strong position on a ridge called Champion Hill, roughly halfway between Vicksburg and Jackson. The ridge stretched for nearly four miles and placed the Confederate troops some seventy feet above their attackers.

The two armies collided on the morning of May 16 in what a Union officer called "one of the most obstinate and murderous conflicts of the entire war." Although the Union army outnumbered the Confederates 29,000 to 20,000, the Confederates had the advantage of shooting down on the attacking Union troops. James McPherson's Union force attacked Pemberton's right wing, while Federals under General John McClernand advanced against the left.

McClernand seemed unnecessarily cautious in pressing his advance, but McPherson's men pushed back the Confederate flank in a bloody fight at close range. A news correspondent reported that "the rattle of musketry was incessant for hours. Cannons thundered til the heavens seemed bursting. Dead men, and wounded, lay strewn everywhere."

Losses were heavy on both sides. About 3,800 Confederate soldiers were killed, wounded, or missing—nearly one out of every five in the battle. Union losses were considerably less—about 2,400 total. Grant was pleased with the victory, but furious at McClernand. He was convinced that if McClernand had pressed the Union advantage, Pemberton would have been forced to surrender and the campaign for Vicksburg would be over.

Pemberton's men retreated to the Big Black River, where they had another good defensive position at a bridge. The Union soldiers pushed after them and McClernand's corps reached the Big Black River on May 17. When McClernand again was reluctant to attack, one of his brigades took matters into their own hands. Without waiting for orders, they rushed the bridge and quickly overtook the Confederates, taking more than 1,000 prisoners.

As Pemberton led his men in a rapid retreat, he received one more message from Johnston: "If it is not too late, evacuate Vicksburg. . . . Save your army and move to the northeast."

But it *was* too late. Pemberton knew he had no choice but to withdraw his beaten troops into their Vicksburg trenches. A Vicksburg woman described the return of Pemberton's men: "Wan, hollow-eyed, ragged, footsore, bloody, the men limped along unarmed. . . followed by siege guns, ambulances, gun-carriages, and wagons in aimless confusion."

Challenging Vicksburg

General Grant finally had his army in position to attack Vicksburg from the east. His daring plan continued to unfold successfully. In the seventeen days since he had led his troops across the Mississippi, they had marched 180 miles, fought and won 5 engagements against separate Confederate forces, and inflicted 7,200 casualties, while suffering 4,300.

Grant and his men were encouraged about the progress they had made since the dark days of winter. The men wanted to keep going—to attack the Confederates in their entrenched position. The only alternative was to lay siege to the city—literally to surround the city and starve the defenders into surrender. Grant hated the idea of a long siege, especially during the broiling Mississippi summer. He also reasoned that Pemberton's men would be exhausted and discouraged, in no condition to fight another battle.

Grant ordered the attack for the morning of May 19, barely twenty-four hours after the Confederates had returned to their bunkers. The Confederates quickly proved that Grant was wrong in thinking they were not prepared for battle. Once they were within their bunkers, their confidence was restored, and they met each Union assault with a firestorm of musket fire and cannon blasts. A Union officer wrote of the attack by his brigade: "What a charge it was! . . . My men came on so gallantly. . . . We did all mortal men could do—but such slaughter!" Seeing his men being cut down by the withering fire, Grant ordered a withdrawal.

★
On May 19, Grant's Union troops attacked Vicksburg and were met with Rebel gunfire and artillery blasts.
★

21

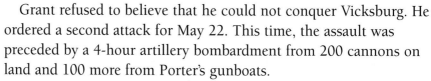
Grant refused to believe that he could not conquer Vicksburg. He ordered a second attack for May 22. This time, the assault was preceded by a 4-hour artillery bombardment from 200 cannons on land and 100 more from Porter's gunboats.

At exactly 10 A.M., the Union men attacked along a three-mile front. Once again, the Confederates poured musket and cannon fire into their attackers. Some defenders lit the fuses on explosive cannon shells and rolled them down the steep hillside into a mass of Union troops. An Indiana soldier described the attack:

> *Every experienced soldier awaited the signal. It came, and in a moment the troops sprang forward. . . . Twenty thousand muskets and 150 cannons belched forth death and destruction. . . Our ranks were becoming decimated. . . The charge was a bloody failure.*

Grant again had to admit defeat, and called off the attack. The Union losses were staggering: 502 killed, 2550 injured, and 147 missing; Confederate losses were only about 500 killed, wounded, and missing combined. Grant's official report concluded: "The nature of the ground about Vicksburg is such that it can only be taken by siege."

The Siege: 47 Days of Torment

Although Grant had not been in favor of a siege, he approached it in his usual thorough way. His men went to work digging trenches, until they had a fifteen-mile network that faced the South's defenses. The men had no regrets about the failed assaults. "They believed they could carry the works in their front," Grant wrote, "and they would not have worked so patiently in the trenches if they had not been allowed to try."

When the siege began, Pemberton's Confederate army of nearly 30,000 faced a Federal force of about 45,000, including two divisions farther east to keep Johnston's troops in check. Now that Grant's army was back close to the Mississippi, supplies and fresh troops were pouring into the camp. Within a few weeks, Grant controlled an army of nearly 75,000 men.

The Biggest Bang

On June 25, 1863, General Grant tried to shorten the siege on Vicksburg in an unusual way. He had some of his troops dig a tunnel from one of their trenches to the Confederate embankments. There, they burrowed under a hill on which the Confederates had a strong gun emplacement. His men then crammed 2,200 pounds of gunpowder into the far end of the tunnel. The general's hope was that an explosion would create a large gap in the Confederate line and that Union troops could rush through before the defenders could recover.

When the signal was given, the fuse was lit, and seconds later a tremendous explosion made the ground tremble for miles in every direction. The power of the blast blew off the top of the hill, replacing it with a crater. Unfortunately for Grant, the Confederates had suspected that the Federals were up to something and had already moved their cannon and trenches farther back. The mission had failed.

★

For weeks in May and June, Union artillery fired nearly 3,000 shells a day into Vicksburg.

★

General Grant's men dug fifteen miles of trenches in preparation for the siege of Vicksburg, which lasted for several weeks.

For the first weeks of the siege, spirits were good among Vicksburg's defenders and the 3,000 civilians who had remained. There was no way to get supplies into the city and no way for anyone to get out. "We were ringed so tight," a soldier recalled, "a cat could not have crept out of Vicksburg without being discovered."

The most difficult part of life under siege in those early weeks was the constant artillery bombardment. Union cannons, including those on the river gunboats, lobbed shells into the defensive lines and the city day and night—as many as 2,800 shells every 24 hours. The mortar shells were the most dangerous, a woman reported in her diary, "for if they explode before reaching the ground, which they generally do, the pieces fly in all directions—the very [smallest] of which will kill one and most of them of sufficient weight to tear through a house from top to bottom!"

For some protection against the bombardment, civilians and soldiers began digging holes and caves in the steep hillsides. Some families moved furniture into their caves, covered the clay floor with oriental carpets, and hung family portraits on the walls. Curtains were used to partition the larger caves into separate rooms.

At first, the besieged residents held out hope that General Johnston would come to their rescue. In a message that Johnston's men managed to get into Vicksburg, he wrote, "I am trying to gather a force which may attempt to relieve you. Hold on." He did manage to increase his Rebel force army to nearly 25,000, but never felt he had enough men to attack Grant's growing army.

As the days passed with no relief in sight, Southern spirits began to sag. Food supplies dwindled to the vanishing point. Mule meat and

dried corn became the standard diet. By mid-June, after nearly a month of siege, even the expressions of hope began to sound desperate, almost frantic. The city's newspaper, now reduced to a single page that was printed on squares of wallpaper, continued to urge readers to "hold out a few days longer, and our lines will be opened, the enemy driven away, the siege raised . . . .The undaunted Johnston is at hand."

The people of Vicksburg did not know that Johnston had already written to President Davis, saying, "I consider saving Vicksburg to be hopeless." Davis urged him not to give up. The president wanted Johnston to get a message to Pemberton to try a breakout. Johnston did send a few probes toward Grant's Union lines, but they quickly reported back that there were no weak spots.

Late in June, Pemberton asked his officers if the men were strong enough to try a breakout. He knew the answer before they reported. The Rebel soldiers had been on one-quarter rations for weeks and nearly half were on the army sicklist. On June 28, he received an anonymous letter from his force stating, among other things, that "this army is now ripe for mutiny unless it can be fed."

The streets of Vicksburg reflected the growing despair. "Palatial residences were crumbling into ruins," a soldier recalled. "Fences were torn down, and houses pulled to pieces for firewood. . . The stores, the few that were open, looked like the ghost of more prosperous times." Another wrote that "danger had long since ceased to cause fear. . . Exploding shells and whistling bullets attracted but little notice."

On July 3, 1863, Union men in the front trenches reported that white flags were showing above the Confederate parapets. The men held their fire as two Confederate horsemen rode slowly to the Union lines. They had a letter from General Pemberton to General Grant asking for a cease-fire to arrange terms for the surrender of Vicksburg.

Grant agreed to the cease-fire and the two generals met that afternoon. Pemberton balked at Grant's demand for an unconditional surrender. He wanted certain conditions for his men, especially the officers. The two men angrily turned away from each other and the negotiations seemed to be over. But aides on both sides stepped in and Grant was finally persuaded to write out a few more lenient

★
Pemberton received a note on June 28 warning him that his Rebel troops were near mutiny.
★

To protect themselves from the Union's constant barrage of shells, many civilians and soldiers in Vicksburg hid inside caves and holes they dug in hillsides.

★

Vicksburg fell on July 4, 1863.

★

terms for the Confederates. The surrender would take place the next day—July 4, Independence Day.

During the cease-fire, men on both sides climbed out of their bunkers and approached each other. Within minutes, they were trading news and looking for relatives or friends among the soldiers of the other side. A private recalled that "several brothers met, and any quantity of cousins. It was a strange scene."

On the morning of July 4, 1863, Vicksburg's defenders stacked their weapons and left their stations. The negotiated terms were that the Confederates would not become prisoners of war and would not be sent to prison camps in the North. Instead, each soldier and officer signed a "parole"—a statement promising to return to his home and not to take up arms again. In addition, Grant permitted each officer to take his horse and his sidearms, a sword and revolver.

As the Southerners marched out after signing their paroles, the Northerners treated them with great respect. There were no cheers of victory, no taunts of the defeated. Many Union soldiers shared their rations with the half-starved Confederate men. A woman wrote: "What a contrast [these] stalwart, well-fed men, so splendidly set up and acoutered [were] to . . . the worn men in gray, who were being blindly dashed against this embodiment of modern power."

The siege of Vicksburg was ended. Including battle casualties, the South had lost roughly 40,000 men in the campaign. They had also surrendered nearly 200 cannons and 60,000 small arms. Most importantly, Vicksburg was now in Union hands.

"The Fate of the Confederacy"

Five days after the surrender of Vicksburg, the Confederate defenders of Port Hudson also laid down their arms. The Union now controlled the entire length of the Mississippi River. President Lincoln, in one of his most famous statements, put it this way: "The Father of Waters again goes unvexed to the Sea."

One result of the victory at Vicksburg was that Grant emerged as the North's greatest battlefield hero. It seemed only a matter of time before Lincoln would ask him to take control of the Union army in the East in order to defeat General Robert E. Lee and his Confederate Army of Northern Virginia.

President Lincoln wrote a letter of praise and apology to his fighting general:

> *I do not remember that you and I ever met personally. I write this now as a grateful acknowledgement for the almost inestimable service you have done this country. . . . When you first reached the vicinity of Vicksburg. . . I never had any faith, except a general hope that you could succeed. . . I now wish to make the personal acknowledgement that you were right, and I was wrong.*

To others, Lincoln wrote that the Vicksburg campaign was "one of the most brilliant in the world." He also made it clear that "Grant is my man, and I am his for the rest of the war."

In his memoirs, Grant wrote, "The fate of the Confederacy was sealed when Vicksburg fell." Though this statement may seem a grand claim, especially since the war continued for nearly two more years, the surrender of Vicksburg was indeed one of the most decisive events of the war.

On the same day that Pemberton surrendered, General Lee was leading his battered army away from Gettysburg, Pennsylvania, after losing the three-day Battle of Gettysburg, the bloodiest battle of the

"I write this now as a grateful acknowledgement for the almost inestimable service you have done this country."

—A letter from President Lincoln to General Grant

The Big Guns

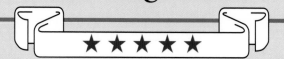

Most military historians agree that powerful and more accurate weapons were one reason that the Civil War was the deadliest war of the nineteenth century. Advances in power and accuracy made the big guns of the Civil War—the artillery—fearsome weapons for both sides. Nowhere were big guns more intimidating than during the siege of Vicksburg.

In the decade before the Civil War, the technique of rifling—cutting grooves inside the barrel of an artillery piece to spin the projectile as it was fired—meant that artillery could shoot farther with greater accuracy than ever before.

Artillery, then as now, is divided into three main categories:

Guns, also called **cannons**, are long-barreled weapons that use large powder charges to fire in a relatively flat arc. Civil War cannons were named for the weight of the shot they fired. The most widely used cannons were six-, twelve-, and twenty-four-pound guns.

Howitzers have short barrels and fire shot or shells with a higher elevation. A standard twelve-pound howitzer could fire a shell more than half a mile.

Mortars are large stubby weapons that fire heavy projectiles in a high arc. When mortar shells

war. Lee's Army of Northern Virginia was not destroyed, but the remaining troops barely managed to make it back to Virginia. Lee's great gamble of carrying the war into the North had failed.

during the battle, however, was a Confederate howitzer nicknamed "Whistling Dick."

This howitzer was originally a smooth bore weapon. When the war broke out, Confederate gunsmiths rifled the barrel of the gun to increase its range. But the grooves cut into the barrel were not precise. This flaw gave shells it fired a slight wobble, which in turn produced an eerie whistling sound with each shot. "Whistling Dick" was part of Vicksburg's river defenses and is credited with sinking the Federal gunboat *Cincinnati* during the siege.

exploded, fragments weighing as much as ten or twenty pounds destroyed anyone or anything within a wide area.

Federal troops used howitzers on land and mounted on gunboats during the siege of Vicksburg. Perhaps the most famous artillery piece used

The North's triumph at Gettysburg, combined with the fall of Vicksburg, made the eventual defeat of the Confederacy nearly certain. As a member of Jefferson Davis's cabinet stated: "The

On July 4, 1863, Confederate soldiers stacked their guns and left their stations.

Confederacy totters to its destruction." And President Davis declared, "We are now in the darkest hour of our political existence."

In the press reports of 1863, and in the popular imagination then and now, Gettysburg has appeared as the more significant of the two battles. It certainly contained within its three days much of what was so extraordinary about the Civil War, including the amazing bravery and honor of the combatants in the midst of America's costliest war as well as the horror of battle. Vicksburg was less dramatic, its horror drawn out in weeks of bombardment and starvation, yet it seems to be symbolic of Grant's role in the war—not flashy, but ferociously committed to winning.

Bruce Catton, a leading Civil War historian, offers this concluding thought:

> *If Gettysburg is what took the eye, Vicksburg was probably more important . . . Vicksburg broke the Confederacy into halves, gave the Mississippi Valley to the Union, and inflicted a wound that would ultimately prove mortal.*

Glossary

artillery weapons, such as cannons, mortars, and howitzers used for discharging large projectiles

bunkers small sand holes or pits

cease-fire an agreement to stop fighting between opponents in order to discuss peace terms

flotilla a small fleet

parapets earthen or stone embankments protecting soldiers from enemy fire

scurvy a disease caused by lack of vitamin C, characterized by bleeding gums and extreme weakness

siege the surrounding and blockading of a city, town, or fortress by an army attempting to capture it

skirmishes minor or preliminary conflicts or disputes

For More Information

Books

Fraser, Mary Ann. *Vicksburg: The Battle That Won the Civil War.* New York: Henry Holt and Company, Inc., 1999.

Graves, Kerry A. *The Civil War* (America Goes to War). Mankato, MN: Bridgestone Books, 2001.

Savage, Douglas J. *Ironclads and Blockades in the Civil War* (World History of the Civil War). New York: Chelsea House, 2000.

Sullivan, George. *The Civil War at Sea.* Brookfield, CT: Twenty First Century Books, 2001.

Web Sites

The Siege of Vicksburg
   Read more about the battle of Vicksburg and the people who fought—
   www.civilwarhome.com/siegeofvicksburg.htm

Vicksburg National Military Park
   Learn more about the Vicksburg battlefield—
   www.nps.gov/vick/

Index